T0196911

A Living Witness

The Journal Writing of My Life, Healing, and God

Craig Wiggins

authorHOUSE®

AuthorHouse™
1663 Liberty Drive
Bloomington, IN 47403
www.authorhouse.com
Phone: 1 (800) 839-8640

Published by AuthorHouse 10/24/2015

ISBN: 978-1-5049-5797-7 (sc)
ISBN: 978-1-5049-5798-4 (e)

Print information available on the last page.

Dedication

To all those who ever felt unloved, unaccepted,
or ostracized, this book is for you.

Acknowledgements

First and foremost I want to thank God for truly blessing me with the gift of word if used wisely can have a profound impact in people's lives. My late mother for sacrificing her time, love, and energy over the years despite our differences. Minister Branch for always keeping me in her thoughts and prayers when I thought it was all over. Evangelist Harper for speaking to me one Sunday afternoon in church after service concluded in September 2001, when the Holy Spirit told her to tell me to write about my life. Pastor Atiba Moses, Mother Vivian Spencer, and Bishop Tolliver- Perrian of the Resuscitated Church Ministries. My friend Purcell Nurse who gave me a piece of the missing puzzle to help me start the writing process. Finally the angels God bestowed in my life for a season and for a lifetime.

Foreword

A Living Witness: The Journal Writing of My Life, Healing, and God is an autobiographical memoir I wrote from September 2001 until December 2001. It chronicles not only my internal struggles, thoughts, and emotions but opened my eyes about the society I live in that shaped my individuality.

"Someone was hurt before you; wronged before you; beaten before you; humiliated before you; raped before you; yet someone SURVIVED". – Maya Angelou

Chapter 1

September 16, 2001,

Today was a beautiful, blessed day in church with the Lord. I arrived there late, but I was still able to hear a good sermon. This week has been horrible for all Americans, and people around the world incredulously witnessing the destruction of the World Trade Center caused by terrorists. This nation is going through so much chaos, and turmoil from A to Z. Rumors of riots in Muslim American neighborhoods who were perceived as the real culprits have run rampant in New York City. Now the United States are thinking about war against Afghanistan, and other countries that were part of the plot. Even worst, Arab and Muslim Americans are being racially and religiously profiled fueled of bias attacks in the United States. People who attack other people in this country are no better than those monsters who killed the people on those planes crashing them. Why do we have so much hatred in our world? There is discrimination and, prejudice because of one's race, religion, gender, ethnicity, sexual orientation, HIV status, ageism, disability, etc. The list continues in our daily interactions as human beings. We are all children of God made in his image and likeness. God made each of us different to love, not to hate. God wants us to bless us unconditionally, but how is that going to happen when we cannot love each other as brothers and sisters? No one deserves to be discriminated, and ostracized. Our children are growing up learning ignorance, intolerance, and hate. God only knows what I'd experience as a child growing up with all kind of abuses. This led me contemplating suicide because I couldn't bear the pain and suffering no more from certain family members. Despite it all, I pray, and ask God to continue to heal me everywhere I hurt because the tears are overwhelmingly burdensome. I was watching Sinead O' Connor's biography on VH1's Behind the Music relating to her story as she spoke of her childhood physical, sexual abuse, and depression. Most importantly I was moved how God saved and delivered her from the torments of her traumatic childhood. God is healing me everywhere I hurt, and I'm going to take it one day at a time.

Chapter 2

September 17, 2001,

Today was a good day for me as I went to Manhattan looking for possible employment that might be of interest. There were people taking pictures of the location where the World Trade Center once stood. One man was angry and started cursing at the crowd because people we're not moving. Another man responded to another individual of the man's profanity, and even stared cursing himself. I traveled mostly in the city until I got off at 14th Street/ Union Square where they had this beautiful memorial for all the victims who died in the building and planes. It was so moving, and touching to see people coming together as one, I was transfixed mentally, emotionally, and spiritually. After the exquisite experience, I went to Brooklyn and exited off on Jay Street/ Borough Hall. I purchased two bottles of water and a book titled, "Soulmates: An Illustrated Guide to Black Love, Sex, and Romance" by Eric V. Copage. Movies like "Waiting to Exhale", "Love Jones", "The Best Man", "The Brothers", and the number one comedy, "Two Can Play That Game" starring Vivica A. Fox, and Morris Chestnut, there is such a dramatic shift now on how African-Americans are portrayed in the movies. Black love, romance, and sex is now comically portrayed with humor, and candor. We should always see the beauty, and resilience that lies in us and not dictated to what the media say we are. I'm better than that!

Chapter 3

September 18, 2001,

I woke up early this morning to the awakening sounds of my grandmother asking me about my job. I'm currently looking for another job because God said he was going to bless me with one. I went to the city to see if they had employment services in newspapers and magazines picking up the periodicals. I went to Queens to see if a restaurant had the same newspaper they had before with all the jobs. The man told me they ran out of them. I went to a drugstore looking for a product dealing with my nails and face. This nice lady told me to go to the pharmacy where they had in the back of the store, I asked the man about my nail and he wrote the name of the product on paper. Later on I asked another man about something for my face, and wrote it discreetly on a piece of paper. Both must be prescribed by my doctor so I definitely got a great head start. I opened my mail and I received a confirmation letter from Pastor Dan Stewart. He's been writing to me over the past two years. God sent him in my life to help me of my hurt and pain. People think they know me, and have the right to judge when they don't know anything about my situation. I know a good judge who always tells me, "I'd won and case closed". You see when you put your trust, and faith in God about things, life, enemies he will make a way for you to win, and never lose. I love God because he made me just the way I am. I will not let ignorant people get the best of me because God is my refuge and strength in the time of trouble. After years of abuse, and the burdens I had to carry

I'm finally learning to love myself. I still have demons to conquer that need disappearing in my life. I have physical, mental, and emotional scars that need healing. I just hope and pray God will help me get to the place that he wants me to be. That will always be my prayer.

Chapter 4

September 19, 2001,

Today was a beautiful, sunny day as I ventured out doing what I had to do. Quieting my thoughts listening to CD101.9 burning incense in my room, I know my day was truly blessed. I went to Harlem today to see this prophetess who is helping me with the things in my life, but she was not there. Psychics really get a bad name because people think most of them are con artists. I gave this woman $140.00 last Friday, and she still has not returned from her "trip. I went to another psychic charging me $10.00 telling me about myself. The research she need to do for the person I'm interested in is $200.00. After I left, I said to myself no. There are some people who are blessed with this gift, but are not using it the right way. I went to this African bookstore I picked up an application for employment, then I was in Fort Greene Park speaking to this woman of being an African- American homeowner. She referred me to a man that was sitting on the bench that she spoke to. We were talking about the high prices of apartments and studios in Brooklyn. I went further up the hill where I spoke to this brother. We had an engaging conversation about music, different forms of writing, and songwriting. He was really nice and open to share his talents with his guitar playing singing. Spiritually, I felt connected to his music and my emotions. Love is something I need now in my life at age 20. For twenty years I lived in fear, blame, guilt, forgiveness, shame, and most importantly being unloved. I want to be loved by someone. I know God loves me, but a soulmate would really be nice. In the 1997 box office hit movie, "Soul Food", Vanessa L.

Williams character, Teri Joseph after finding out her husband's infidelity, she tells Myles, "Everything I love, I lose". As for me, I feel this way trying to have unconditional love, peace, and happiness in my life. Can I imagine? Yes, because I know it is real. I hope and pray God will send me the right one I would love to share my world.

Chapter 5

September 20, 2001,

A rainy day filled the earth as I quietly spent some time at home. My grandmother wanted m to go to the store for her to buy bananas. Later on I was watching a fashion show on television showcasing African-American models and fashion designers. It's always good seeing black people doing positive things. It makes me proud to do anything I want to do in life if I set my mind to it. I ran across a neighbor who will ask me for money or anyone else. I feel if God gave you two hands, legs, two feet, and a brain, then do something with it. Get a job! I'm not going to let his ignorance or anyone else get to me. Of course, he used the word "nigga", but that show how ignorant and immature he is for twenty-six. The evening concluded watching BET's Comicview, and the show before that, "Oh Drama"! Oh Drama had excellent guests such as comediennes Chocolate, Hope, Sheryl Underwood, and Dr. Juanita Bynum. (Her article was featured in the May 2001 issue of Essence). As well as hostesses Kym Whitley, Vanessa Bell Calloway, and Julissa Martinez. The topic was about God, being saved, and how you should live right as a Christian. The topic caught my attention with the women giving their own opinions reflecting myself in different ways. People think a Christian is suppose to be holy, holy, holy. None of us in this world is perfect except God. For the bible says, "All have sinned falling short to the glory of God". God is good all the time and I want to be perfect all the time, but its humanly impossible. I try to live up to perfection knowing I don't live in a stain free world.

Chapter 6

September 21, 2001,

Today was a hot, humid day as I went to my job to pick up my paycheck. I was working, and still am as a telemarketer before the horrific incident, and tragedy of September 11. The good Lord blessed me with fourteen hours on my check instead of twelve because I work twelve hours a day. I bought a shirt that read, "God Bless America" showing the World Trade Center 1975-2001. I felt proud wearing that because it shows patriotism and respect of the American symbol. My grandmother, and cousin were talking about the crisis, and possibly being drafted. In my mind, I thought, "hell no". I'd been through enough wars in my young life as it is, and I did not want to be bothered with any kind of negative situations. The evening concluded watching the program of celebrities coming together from Brad Pitt to Julia Roberts, to Chris Rock, and Cuba Gooding, Jr. I just hope and pray this too shall come to pass.

Chapter 7

September 22, 2001,

Today was a blessed day which I gave thanks to my Lord and Savior Jesus Christ. It started with ironing my clothes so I can meet my counselor for advice and support. My church was also saying goodbyes to my dear friend and missionary board member Sister Dorothy Thompson. She is a wonderful, beautiful, spirited person inside out. My church is truly blessed because God brought my church through tough times. It's 2001, the new millennium for changes in my life as well as myself. It's great to have God in your life and still enjoy the best things with joy. I want to have a whole new change about myself inside out. God is going to make my dreams come true. He's going to bless me with a soulmate, be prosperous in all I do, and have a whole new physical appearance. It's time for a change though it won't be easy. I have to try.

Chapter 8

September 23, 2001,

The blessings of God are beautiful as I enjoyed an awesome day in service. My neighbor Dana asked about me as she always is and came over informing me that one of his sisters in the church was looking for me. She gave me some nice casual shoes I tried on and it was though that counts. I decided to go train hopping taking the number 4 to Fordham Road in the boogie down Bronx. I started feeling tired, and went home to enjoy the rest of the evening reflecting on how God was good to me. I'm trying to be a good person, but I always know someone is always looking out for my best interest.

Chapter 9

September 25, 2001,

It was a cloudy, rainy day that affected my mood. I didn't have any money to go to work. I asked my grandmother for money, but she only gave me four dollars. I needed more than that for food. It turned into an argument, and I don't understand why? I beg her if she can give me twenty dollars which she finally did. Why do my grandmother and almost every family member act like I'm the worst person in the world? They don't know what I'd been dealing in my life. When I tell them next thing you know they use it to hurt me, but personally 2001 was a horrific year for me, but I'm being optimistic, hopefully, and most importantly prayerful that 2002 will be better. Later on that evening, I attended bible study, and my bishop asked me, "Do you like you're blessed?" I responded yes I am.

Chapter 10

September 26, 2001,

Today I went for a job interview that went really well. God blessed me to be and feel confident, and to put all my trust and faith in him. The job pays $10-$20 per hour which is excellent and I'll also be doing marketing, but it won't be setting. I'll be telling people how to save on their energy bills. I hope and pray that God will bless me with a better paying job, and give me favor on my credit report, wealth, and be prosperous. I don't want to focus on the material things because my spiritual stability is extremely important. Without the Lord, I'm nothing. Tonight I watched my favorite show, "Soul Food". The series is taking a hiatus but in the meantime, I have to convey myself with priorities that are crucially beneficial to me.

Chapter II

September 27, 2001,

I went on my day of observation in reference seeing on how the marketing job works. You tell people on how they can save money on their energy bill. I went with this seventeen- year-old high school dropout. I'm twenty, but I'm sure glad I don't look my age. I was in the Midwood section of Brooklyn, New York and we were going door to door. I finally couldn't take it anymore, and left him by himself with his stuff that he gave me, and I went home. I know it was wrong, but the Holy Spirit spoke to me about this job not being right for me. Who want to go door to door telling people about something and then get an attitude? I went to church for their evening service for people who are deeply hurting spiritually. I hope I'll be able to stand, and rise above any challenges, but subconsciously it's taking a toll on me.

Chapter 12

October 1, 2001,

I went to my job this morning meeting my other co-workers, but instead I took a trip to the city. What today was the longest, cold, insightful day I'd ever experienced in my life? I know God shows us things in our lives to realize why we see things from happy to sad, to blessed to glad because he spared us from the worst people. I went to Pier 94 on the West Side Highway where survivors and victims' families were trying to get financial assistance. There were so many people, and organizations ranging from The Salvation Army to The American Red Cross, and even spiritual care. A Salvation Army employee told me to go to DeWitt Clinton Park across the street from the Pier 94 site. Other people were there too, but after six hours of eating snacks, drinking three cups of hot chocolate, and apple cider, I finally received services from them. They registered me asking for my information which in hindsight was worth it. The Red Cross is going to send me a check for $321.00 which is a blessing I don't take for granted.

Chapter 13

October 2, 2001,

A beautiful, bright sunny day as I prepared myself to do what I have to do. My mother came over this morning cooking, and assisting my grandmother. She was trying to help me see if I can receive food stamps. Tomorrow, I'm going to Williamsburg, Brooklyn to hopefully receive my benefits. I went to my former college Long Island Univeristy (Brooklyn Campus) to the Registrar's office for them to fill out the bottom part of the paper, so I can receive my loan deferment at approximately six months. I have to payback my loan starting March 2002. What I really need is a personal loan if I can get one due to my bad credit. Where there is God, there will always be a way. My blessed day concluded with once again bible study that simply concluded my evening. Now the real work begins in a matter of hours.

Chapter 14

October 3, 2001,

It sure felt like summertime as I enjoyed the 78 degree weather to my liking. I went to Williamsburg on Marcy Avenue as I applied for assistance. Being unemployed for two weeks you need all the assistance you can, or will receive. I went online to register under Safe Horizon, but that was only for the victims of the World Trade Center, and for the people who lived around the area. I went to the Department of Labor where a lady gave me a phone number to call for assistance, and other jobs I might be interested in. After leaving with a sense of relief waiting for the shuttle bus, another woman gave me information where I can apply for a job. I then went to my native Brooklyn where I applied for a personal loan of $20,000. I hope I can get the loan despite my unattractive credit. I went home seeing my uncle Kevin, and I secretly hate him. He abused me physically and verbally when I was a little boy. I try to escape the evils, pain, and trauma of my childhood, and growing up. I need the scars to go away because people want to see me die.

Chapter 15

October 4, 2001,

I spent time to myself after I left work early due to the technical difficulties in the computers. I might have to look for a job! God help me because you know jobs are hard to find. I like my job because I like the people I work with in my industry. Later in the afternoon, I went home to see if I have any mail, and then I went out in Fort Greene. I like to spend time by myself to get away from people in my life that makes me miserable. Sometimes I hide my pain mentally because of the things I experienced as a child. Physical abuse, mental, and emotional abuse. Not being or feeling loved, raped, traumatized, being a scapegoat, confused about sex and sexuality. I wished and prayed to God that never happened. I don't want to live in this world afraid and lonely. For me the older I got, the worse it was. Do you know what it feel like to be a victim of violence all of your life? Do you know what it feel like to live in fear of a family member who abused you? Do you know what it feel like crying in the middle of the night asking the Lord why people are talking about me in a negative way? It feels horrible! It's a violation of the body, soul, and spirit. It's always been in my life for years. As a child of God, I know the Lord knows my inner thoughts and the pain I still see after all these years. Physical, mental, and emotional scars I wish will disappear. That's where the healing comes in. That's where God come in to heal me everywhere I hurt. Yes it still hurts, but I know in my heart, breakthrough will happen, and even healing around the world. My prayer is to be healed from the scars of my youth, and even now. I want to be happy and finally loved.

Chapter 16

October 5, 2001,

I experienced a day that reminded me of summertime minus feeling a bit chilly. I only worked today for a couple of hours. My supervisor along with his girlfriend and myself went to Greenwich Village. It was fun and for the first time in my life, I really felt I was in a clique. Like I really belong to something and it felt good. My grandmother is spending a few days with my mother. As that was happening, I went uptown in Harlem for hip-hop community forum and a MC battle. One of the speakers was Kevin Powell, a young, intelligent African-American writer, journalist, and activist. The forum was insightful, uplifting, and enlightening. After the event concluded, I bought a Jamaican dish, and I went home. I later saw my neighbor and friend Roberta celebrating Friday nights with her friend Natalie. Tomorrow is another day, and I thank God for blessing this one.

Chapter 17

October 6, 2001,

Dealing with my grandmother being absent from home I was getting use to being alone. Loneliness has always been a part of me. I feel like an outcast in my family. My family treats me like I'm the worst person in the world. I sacrifice myself so many times so much I dropped out of school due to the stress, and not liking the school at all. The more I did, the less I received. My pain, anger, hurt, fear, and loneliness was due to the abuses I endured as a child. No one don't know the real me. I had to pretend to people I was happy when I was putting a smiling façade. When I was born, my father left my mother and I, fourteen years later in 1995, I gone through another trauma, being viciously assaulted by a group of boys because I was trying to be a peacemaker between my sister and a former friend. In the meantime you're always getting beat up by Kevin who has this violent rage, but always running to church every Sunday. When your sister doesn't even acknowledge that you're a human being, and a brother who risked his life trying to protect her from getting killed. That hurts! Scars are so painful, and leave you victimized for a long time. I'm not angry at God because I love him, and he will always be there for me. He always knew I had low self-esteem because of the things that happened in my life. I want to finish college, and live my dreams. I'm trying to help and love myself each day. It's a hard struggle, but I know for sure God has an awesome, beautiful plan in my life.

Chapter 18

October 7, 2001,

It was a shocking day for me to listen and accept. I'm tired of Kevin physically, verbally, and mentally abusing, and bullying me. He was renovating the bathroom downstairs with my former neighbor and friend Terry when I heard him talk about me in a nasty way. I was so angry that I wanted to curse him out, and him to pay for what he did to me all of these years. No one understands me in the physical realm, but spiritually I knew God had already seen enough. Will I ever be happy in my life? Will this abuse continue to go on? I can't live like this anymore and its killing me. Kevin is a monster full of evil and hatred of me. I don't know what to do about this situation, but I wish I can run away from everyone. This is a living nightmare for me.

Chapter 19

October 8, 2001,

After what happened, and again shocked of what I heard, I stayed in my room for most of the day. My mother came over this morning telling me about my grandmother, and making sure she's okay. Her home attendant was there, and I helped her with what needed to be done. I was in the room by myself angry, tired of being treated this way after all these years. Years of living hell and misery I'd endured in my childhood, and in my life. I saw Kevin outside with my grandmother helping her and I went downstairs, opened the door, and I was trying to keep the middle door open. It didn't work, and his talking to me got me aggravated which subsequently ended with fighting. My neighbor Roberta and Terry had to hold me back trying to keep the peace. I was in her house crying to her about what I'd been dealing with and I was tired. Tired of the pain, and suffering brought upon him. No one gave me a chance to listen to my feelings, and how I felt. No matter how I try to impress my family, or anyone else, it's never good enough. I'm hurting inside and the only one who is helping me is God. Terry tells me my uncle want me to come back home after he threatened to kick me out which is not his house, and apologize to him and my grandmother. For what? I thought about it, but reluctantly I did. People can beat me up with words and fist, but I know I will not give up because I know my change will come. All of those people whether they were related to me or not are going to regret what they did to me. You reap what you sow!

Chapter 20

October 9, 2001,

My prayers were answered today as I set out to help my grandmother anyway I can. This morning I cooked her breakfast, and I spent most of my time all day with her. I'm always running away from the house. I didn't have any breakfast for myself, so I went to McDonald's. I saw Kevin, and he told me to pick up the weeds in the backyard which I did. Terry came by to help him with work, and later on that evening, I went to bible study. I didn't get approved for the loan, but God knows best, and when the time is right, then we will see what happens. I don't know what the future holds for an unpleasant 2001, but I'll be glad when it's over.

Chapter 21

October 10, 2001,

Nothing really much to do as I continue to keep myself open being more mindful, gentler, and open helping my grandmother, and mother with what they have to do. I went to the Chinese store, and bought my mother and I soup and crackers. We were watching the 1980 movie, "Gloria", starring Academy-Award nominated actress Gena Rowlands. I went to Manhattan if I can get more financial help at Pier 94 on the West Side Highway. I was inside the building; I saw those who were missing from the World Trade Center tragedy. The world healing more than before. All this hatred has got to stop because if it doesn't, we're always going to live in terror. God loves us so much! It's a shame we don't even love each other, and most importantly ourselves.

Chapter 22

October 15, 2001,

Today was a beautiful, sunny Monday as I went job hunting spending quality time in New York City. I went to One Police Plaza where I submitted my resume for City Custodial Agent. They're going to notify me in the mail to see if I qualify. Picked up my last paycheck last week, but I'm not happy where I work at. I hope God bless me with a job that has good pay, and pays the bills. I went to 110th Street in Harlem walking through the beauty of Central Park. It was like a magical forest with big bamboo trees illuminating the air in all its majestic glory. The closest thing to heaven I'll ever get spending precious times and spiritual moments with the Lord.

Chapter 23

October 16, 2001,

I was fired from my job today because I cursed a customer who told me, "Fuck you", and I was not going to tolerate verbal abuse. My boss care about making money, and his lousy business struggling to stay competitive. I refuse to sell my soul to anyone in this world just to make them like me. Being a telemarketer is not easy, but nevertheless my other supervisor Frank did not want to let me go. I wanted to leave the job anyway! I'm hurt, and angry, but I know my heavenly father will help me get to the place where I should be. It can be psychologically stressful, but I need to get back in the work force.

Chapter 24

October 17, 2001,

Today was a decent, and weird day as I went for a job interview in Brooklyn for a mailroom position. A woman told me the positions were already full, but there were job openings in Manhattan. I have to be at my job this Saturday from noon until 8 p.m. which will be my working hours. I was standing outside a big crowd on 34th Street for the job fair at Madison Square Garden. I submitted my resumes to two men who were nice to other people who had also lost their jobs. I saw people as I tried to get out of the area yelling, screaming, and cursing at each other. I had my own incident when I was on the number 6 train, and these two boys from different nationalities kept looking at me, and laughing like I had two heads. I asked him, "Is anything funny"? The boy replied, "No, I wasn't laughing at you"? People get on my nerves, but I'm glad to speak up for myself, and not allow people intimidate me.

Chapter 25

October 18, 2001,

The Lord blessed me with a brand new job working in the mailroom which was my first day on the job. The best part about my job is benefits. I was always searching for a job with benefits. Thank you Jesus! My working hours will be five days a week Monday through Friday from 7 a.m. until 3 p.m. I'm listening to Mary J. Blige's new album, "No More Drama" which definitely speaks to me. One of her songs is a beautiful, upbeat, tempo called "Testimony". I love Mary, and I can relate to her pain, and her struggles. She's a kindred spirit, and as I'm listening to her lyrics, my spirit is moved by her words. I'm so happy for her, and I pray God will always continue to bless her with her singing, and career. I'm still going through my healing process in the meantime feeling a little better. There's still work that need to be done. Listen to her words, "It's gonna be alright, everything will be okay. This is my testimony. Mary's story. Trouble don't last always". Amen!

Chapter 26

October 20, 2001,

I went to work today which I almost didn't make it on time. I hailed a cab to take me to Jay Street (Borough Hall). I got out of the cab to catch the F train, but I didn't see it so I took the A train. Now I thought the A stopped at 23rd Street, but boy was I wrong. I got off on 34th Street walking down Eighth Avenue until I hit my destination, West 26th Street. I left work early which was good, but I only had four dollars left! When I arrived home, I checked my mail, and I saw my check from the American Red Cross for $321.00. Thank God! Just what I needed in the nick of time. Thank you, Heavenly Father for the money you gave me, and I will tithe the money you blessed me with. I'm so happy, I could be the spokesperson for Kool-Aid.

Chapter 27

October 21, 2001,

Church was good as God poured his spirit this morning. It was such a good day earlier this morning, I finally went food shopping budgeting myself at least $40.00. I tithe ten percent of my paycheck, and it felt good as well as the service. Today's sermon was, I Want to Go to the Next Level". I know in my mind, heart, soul, and spirit, that he wants me to go there, and I accept. After the service, I greeted my brothers, and sisters, and went downtown to get a few items. The church was having another service at four, and even though I arrived late, I still made it on time. God is always meeting me at the appointed hour no matter how early or late I arrive.

Chapter 28

October 22, 2001,

Today was a good day at my job. I got up at 5:45 a.m., and went straight to work. My eyes were starting to feel tired, but as I got through the day, I started to feel better. Financially, I hope this will help me to pay all of my debts because having a bad credit is very difficult to get out of. I was watching the beautiful, talented spirit of the late Aaliyah's videos, "Rock the Boat", and "Are You That Somebody". It seems so surreal that she's gone, but I know that she and the late R&B singer Phyllis Hyman (who passed away in June 1995), will always be angels in our hearts and minds forever. Rest in peace to Aaliyah, and Phyllis Hyman.

Chapter 29

October 24, 2001,

Today was a day that goes well in the being, but start to not go well later on. When I was working, I told this lady, I'm not working as a mail sorter, I'm an examiner. Because of the fear of people opening their mail due to Anthrax, a powder that gets on people's skin which can lead to death. She started getting an attitude about it, and I'm so tired of people, and their nonsense. I probably be in jail right now for assault because this year has been horrible. Fighting everyone in my life, and people's attitude, I'm sick of it all. I wish I'd never gone through the bad things, and people I'd experience in my life. It's sad but undeniably true.

Chapter 30

November 1, 2001,

It was a splendid day as I went to work getting to know the other co-workers from the 2-10 p.m. shift. One of them I met was Becky who was in her late forties with a lively spirit, and wonderful personality. We had lunch together, and we were talking about what we want to do with our lives. Immediately, I knew that she, and I was going to have a fun, cool relationship together as co-workers and friends. I'm truly blessed to be working with some perks, and giving me favor which I'm still learning about what it mean. In my church, I'm in the Shepherd's ministry which was started by Sister Melissa Slater. I hope I'll continue to receive everything with my name on it, and be healed everywhere I hurt. It's something that has to be worked on daily. I'm not rushing about it at all.

Chapter 31

November 5, 2001,

One of my co-workers started asking me very uncomfortable questions which was making me very angry inside, but I kept my composure. I'm starting to have second thoughts about my job because the people I'm around are so immature, and disrespectful. One of them have a bad case of halitosis! I been finding solace in getting professional help from my therapist Zack Miller. He really understands me as a person, and patient. I hope I can see him as long as I can because I have an outlet where I can feel comfortable being in my own skin without fear, or judgment. In the meantime, I'm thinking about that $282.00 a week paycheck, but once again I'm trying to be optimistic around the fools I have to be with at work.

Chapter 32

November 10, 2001,

I'm excited about Nicole's birthday party which I bought her Ja Rule's, "Pain Is Love" CD. She was really nervous, but I tried to calm her down to the best of my ability. A lot of people were there even my sister, and her friend. I got into a verbal confrontation with this stupid, ignorant guy at the party complaining that he doesn't want me to stand behind him, telling me to move. Excuse me, but who the hell are you to tell me where I should move? I told Nicole's mother what happened and I let it go. It was so hot, and crowded downstairs in the basement, but I made a vow to myself never go to a house party again. It's always some unnecessary drama that should not even happen, but when you deal with immature people that's what is expected. I'm a mature person who has no time to deal with foolishness. This world makes me sick with people's attitude, hatred, and ignorance. They can all go straight to hell.

Chapter 33

November 12, 2001,

Today was Veterans Day as I went to work doing my daily duties. A lot of my co-workers were not there because most of them did not have to come. I need the money, but more than that I need a financial miracle. Working in Chelsea to me is like a whole different world because the diversity is inevitable. When I was a little kid, I had this fantasy of becoming a famous actor, and living in Manhattan. Times change and so do you as a person because everything cannot stay the same. Physically, mentally, emotionally, and spiritually I know, and feel that. I think I'll always will.

Chapter 34

November 13, 2001,

Today was a good, answered prayer day. Later at my job, I'd been catching attitudes, but thank God it's starting to get better. I went shopping Downtown Brooklyn, and bought this beautiful, beige sweater with a scarf for $19.99. Then I went to an African-American bookstore buying a 2002 calendar of the late, great painter Jacob Lawrence. When I was in college, I did research about him in my English class, and I'd been a fan of his breathtaking paintings ever since. Later in the evening, I received two letters from Pastor Dan Stewart that God sent in my life, and I went to bible study. I spoke to Jessica and she is a wonderful friend, mentor, and prophetess. She's a woman of God I admire and respect.

Chapter 35

December 1, 2001,

Today the nation is observing World Aids Day honoring, and remembering those who are either living with the virus, and those who have succumbed from the disease. I was outside the Adam Clayton Powell Jr State Building in Harlem, New York reading the names of those who passed away. People regardless of age, race, color, religion, and sexual orientation are dying every day, and we need to educate liberating people of the virus. As a society, we have come a long way from being just a gay white man's disease, but there is still a lot of discrimination, stigma, and ignorance against people living with HIV/AIDS. This virus is at war, and shows no mercy unless we continue to come together as one putting away our bigotry, and unite as a people to once and for all eliminate this killer. In Africa, and around the world human beings are dying, and organizations that educate people about HIV/AIDS prevention, hopefully, someday, there will be a cure to heal all of those around the world. With God's love, grace, and mercy, we can and will deliver.

Chapter 36

December 16, 2001,

Thoughts are going through my head as the New Year approaches, and I'm worried of what 2002 has in store for me. It's a constant fear I developed since I graduated from high school. I know that I don't walk in this world alone for God is always with me. Fighting my internal struggles is bad timing especially around the holiday season because depression, and holidays are not the best of friends. I'm trying to keep the faith because that is what has helped me survive the difficult times in my life. I know my life has a purpose, and meaning, but it's a long way down the road to healing, and recovery of my strength that I never knew existed. I know that there is a light at the end of the tunnel. I just know it!

Chapter 37

December 31, 2001,

Today is the last day of the year, and I'm feeling very ambivalent about 2002. It seems within a few hours the new year will be around the corner. Don't get me wrong! I do have a sense of hope and pride that God's blessings will be ready for me any minute. I am trying my best to be hopeful because there is something special when you are with people, who truly love and care about you. I'm attending church tonight, and I'm going to give God all the praise, honor, and glory for letting me see another year transitioning into changes in my life. I have so many dreams, and aspirations to follow that will take me far than I can ever imagine. I hope 2002, and the years to come it will make me stronger in this life. I will have trials, and tribulations, but ultimately someone bigger than you and I will carry me through. May I have a witness?

For more information please contact:

Craig Wiggins

Email: crg_wggns@yahoo.com

Twitter: @peaceandspirit

Facebook.com: Craig Wiggins

Instagram.com: crg_wggns

Printed in the United States
By Bookmasters